ENOUGH

and other magic words

to transform your life

by David W. Jones

Valjean Press, Nashville
David Jones is pastor of
Harpeth Presbyterian Church,
Brentwood, Tennessee
and is also the author of:

The Psychology of Jesus:
Practical Help for Living in Relationship

In the Beginning Were the Words:
A Look at the First Chapters of Genesis
through Poetry

The Enlightenment of Jesus:
Practical Steps to Life Awake

Moses and Mickey Mouse:
How to Find Holy Ground in the
Magic Kingdom and Other
Unusual Places

For the Love of Sophia
Wisdom Stories from Around the World
And Across the Ages

For more information on these books,
go to: www.davidwjonesbooks.com

Contents

Introduction

"Watch this," I said to my son, Nathan.

I let go of his hand, waved my arms, and spoke again, "Open sesame."

The doors parted in front of us like the Red Sea before Moses.

"Cool," said Nathan.

Together we walked, father and son, through the doors and into Target. I was walking tall, confident my four year old son thought me a powerful man, a man above other men, a dad above other dads.

In the check-out line, I pulled coin after coin from his ears and then made them disappear.

At the mall, I raised my arms on a staircase, whispered, "Up," and mysteriously the steps escalated us from the first floor to the second.

On the way home, I wiggled my fingers and whispered, "Change," as the traffic light in front of us transformed from red to green.

"Cool, Dad," Nathan said again.

Yes, my son knew me to be a powerful man, and I loved it.

I have often imagined myself as Merlin, Gandalf, or Dumbledore, and acted out the role, though I must admit most of my attempts at prestidigitation have left audiences over the age of four unimpressed. Even now, at age eight, Nathan finds my attempts at magic only slightly intriguing.

Throughout my life, my efforts to enthrall have brought more amusement than amazement.

At age eight, I was given *The Magic Hat* for Christmas. Apparently Santa shopped on television because I had seen a commercial for the hat, *Brought to you by Ronco, makers of the Ginsu Knife and The Miracle Wrinkle Erase Cream.*

The Magic Hat wasn't like those felt toppers. Hard plastic, it actually hurt a little when you put it on your head. The discomfort did have a pay off for *The Magic Hat* had lots of compartments; the largest was a secret door in the bottom where the rabbit imprinted bandanna lived ready to be pulled out to dazzle any audience. My favorite compartment was the small reservoir beneath the rabbit's home, accessed by a slot in the side. With the hat tilted just right, a small dixie-cup sized pitcher of water could be poured into the hat, and then disappear, safely stored for you to put the hat on your head and astound your audience, just like on the commercial.

As has been my general philosophy much of my life, if a little is good then a lot is great, so I didn't use the tiny pitcher, instead, I used a half gallon jug. In front of grandmother, aunt, uncle, mom, dad, brother and sisters, I poured the water in, and then peered down to see, instead of a dry bottom, a sizeable pond in the bottom of the hat.

I had a tough choice. I could have said, "Oops it didn't work," but in typical style, I went for the comic relief. I put it on my head, and as water poured like Niagara, I said, "Ta-dah."

Even though the magic hat was a magic flop, I didn't stop imagining myself a wizard and dreaming of magical powers.

Through both research and experience, I have discovered that there is pragmatic, practical, applicable magic. No order from Ronco needed, no expensive equipment necessary, just a beginners knowledge of magic words. Yes, magic words do exist, powerful, transforming, magic words.

These words can do more than pull a rabbit (bandanna or furry) from a hat. These words can do more than make an assistant disappear or reappear. These words can erase mistakes, open doors, bring opportunities, form futures, shape new realities, and create life where there was little or no life before. .

Sound absurd?

Before you close this book for another, before you cast aside these pages for a remote control, let me share with you how I've seen magic words change lives.

In August of 1988, I, on bended knee, asked Carrie Jo Richards if she would marry me. With a single word, a simple but powerful *yes*, both of our lives changed. *Yes* was definitely a transforming magic word for us.

Just under a year later, in front of a congregation on the coast of South Carolina, and in front of her father, a preacher, we said, *I do.* With these two words we changed from single individuals into a couple, a family, *two people but one life before us* was what her father said. Though we may not have looked different at that moment, God, her father, the church, and the United States of America said that we were, "husband and wife," all from two magic words, *I do.*

I have seen magic words change the lives of others in a courtroom. "Ladies and Gentlemen of the jury, have you reached a verdict?" the judge asked. "We have your honor," replied the foreman. "What say you?"

asked the judge. "We find the defendant not guilty," and an imprisoned teen goes free because the foreman said two magical words, *Not guilty*.

Two hundred plus years ago, the Continental Congress ratified these powerful magic words, *We hold these truths to be self-evident, that all men are created equal...* With those words, and the ones that followed, a nation was formed, a new reality spoken, written, willed into existence, a country was shaped from powerful words, a country which has survived challenge upon challenge, from beyond and from within, for over two centuries. On July 4th, 1776, the representatives of thirteen colonies signed their names to these words, and their lives, your life, and the world was changed.

In this book are more magic words, simple words with great power, words you've heard before, but not until now discovered their might; words which by saying them, you can change your life for the better, transforming your life from dry desert to Eden-like garden, all because you say so.

Each chapter will follow a simple pattern, a pattern followed by every magician in a show:

The problem: In a magic show, before any magic words can be said, before any wand can be waved, there must be a clear and evident problem: an empty hat, a torn paper, a hidden card, an assistant sawn in two, a woman vanished, a wizard chained. The act begins with a problem. The magic makes little sense without the problem.

The magic words: "Abbra Cadabra," "Hocus Pocus," or some other phrase is often said in a magic show. Tricks are usually performed with a word or command, or perhaps there is a nonverbal visual with a wave of wand or hand. Though magicians and wizards don't always use words, they almost always without fail have some show of magic directed at the presented problem.

And finally, there is *the transformation*: Magic results in something unexpected, something new: an empty hat is full of rabbit, a torn newspaper is restored, a woman vanished is returned, or an incarcerated wizard is liberated. There is always a dramatic change as a result of the magic.

In each chapter that follows, I'll use these three simple steps showing our problem, simple magic words, and how the words can result in your transformation.

Still skeptical? Read on. But first, say it with me, *Open sesame...*

Chapter One

I can't get no satisfaction.
Mick Jagger

The Problem

I like stuff.

When we moved in our current home, with more stuff than we could fit into the house, a lot of it went to the attic. At the time I told my wife Carrie, "If we don't use this stuff in the first year, let's get rid of it." She agreed. That was ten years ago. It's still there, plus a lot more, with added floor space. We have a hard time getting rid of our stuff. Our neighbors aren't much different. Drive around our subdivision and you'll see cars in driveways because garages are all full of stuff.

My neighbors and I are not alone in our acquisition and collection of stuff, our hoarding is no neighborhood peculiarity. According to George Carlin, it's our national pastime...

...that's what this country is all about. Tryin' to get more stuff. Stuff you don't want, stuff you don't need, stuff that's poorly made, stuff that's overpriced. Even stuff you can't afford! Gotta keep on gettin' more stuff. Otherwise someone else might wind up with more stuff. Can't let that happen. Gotta have the most stuff...

So now you got a houseful of stuff. And, even though you might like your house, you gotta move. Gotta get a bigger house. Why? Too much stuff! And that means you gotta move all your stuff. Or maybe, put some of your stuff in storage.

Storage! Imagine that. There's a whole industry based on keepin' an eye on other people's stuff.

Or maybe you could sell some of your stuff. Have a yard sale, have a garage sale! Some people drive around all weekend just lookin' for garage sales. They don't have enough of their own stuff, they wanna buy other people's stuff.[1]

Carlin is right. We love stuff. When we want more stuff, we go looking for it, searching for it, shopping. Apparently it's part of our nature.

Read the following from the Bible's first book, the book of Genesis, third chapter, the story of Adam and Eve. Notice how their story is not just the tale of two people long ago but a chronicle of our lives today with insight as timely as George Carlin's commentary.

The Text

Genesis 3: [6] *So when the woman saw that the tree was good for food, and that it was a delight to the eyes, and that the tree was to be desired to make one wise, she took of its fruit and ate; and she also gave some to her husband, who was with her, and he ate.*

Have you ever considered what Adam and Eve were doing when they got into so much trouble? As I read the story, they were shopping. The forbidden fruit was not scattered throughout the garden, not in many places, not in multiple locations, but one place, one site, one location and one location only. Perhaps they just came upon it, "Oh, look, the forbidden fruit..." or,

---

[1] George Carlin, *Brain Droppings*, p. 38

perhaps, they were looking for something, searching, shopping. Somewhere in their dissatisfaction they thought, "If only we had something more..."

Today, if we want *more*, we don't have to wander through a garden, we can go wander through a mall. The mall is a relatively new innovation. Historically, the order went like this: you had a need; you figured out what you wanted to meet the need; you figured out how to pay for it; then you shopped for the right one; and then, and only then, you bought it. Not any more, not with malls and credit cards, for malls aren't about shopping for what you need, malls exist to help you find what you want regardless of need. Now the order is: shop, figure out what you want that you didn't know you wanted before, charge it, get it, and later, figure out how to pay for it. Because shopping isn't about need and instead is about some amorphous unperceived want, some undefined emptiness, if what we buy now doesn't fill it, if what we buy gives us no lasting satisfaction, we buy something else. And now it's even simpler, instead of going to the mall, you don't even have to leave your home to search for what you must have that you didn't even know you wanted – you can search online.

William Sloan Coffin described our problem this way,

There are people and things in this world, and people are to be loved and things are to be used. And it is increasingly important that we love people and use things, for there is so much in our gadget minded, consumer-oriented society that is encouraging us to love things and use people.

As I read and re-read the story of Adam and Eve, I want to scream out, "You're in Eden! Leave the damned apple alone. Don't you have enough? Why do you want *more?*" Yet, every time I read it, they don't seem to hear me. They chase their *more*, their must-have, their desire above other desires, the want they perceive as need, and then all hell breaks loose. For whatever reason, whatever dissatisfaction they perceived, they had to have *more*. Once they saw the fruit, once it appeared *good* to them and was a *delight* to their eyes, they were sure that life with the forbidden fruit was going to be better than life without it, and life without it less than life with it.

Their problems came, simply because they knew *more* and only *more*. What they needed was another word, a magic word...

Enough

The Text Revisited

What if Adam and Eve had known the simple word *enough* and used it at the base of the tree of trouble? Their story would have been much different, much simpler, less painful, something like this... (I've left the original passage from Genesis in italics.)

Genesis 3: *the woman saw that the tree was good for food, and that it was a delight to the eyes, and that the tree was to be desired to make one wise...* but then she said to herself, "What are you thinking? You live in a beautiful garden. This is paradise. You have everything you need to be happy right here. You have *enough*."

She talked with Adam. They contemplated what they needed and what they had. Adam affirmed, "Yes, we have *enough*."

They said it together, "Yes, we have *enough*."

And then the two of them walked away, happy together.

The Transformation

If Adam and Eve had known *enough*, and used it, their lives, their situation, and their relationships all would have been better. But they didn't. However, just because they didn't know *enough*, doesn't mean that you can't. The magic of *enough* is easily accessible. This I know, for I know people who use *enough* often to transform their lives and the lives of their families. For example, my friend Jimmie Manning...

Jimmie has ENOUGH as a customized license plate. He was asked, "Jimmie, would you still have that license plate if someone gave you a new Mercedes?" "Nope," he replied, "then I'd get a plate that says, *More than Enough.*"

Jimmie had the plate made after reading *Life is So Good!*, the biography of George Dawson, a man who signed his name with an X until age 98. At 98 George learned to read and write.

George's biographer asked him, "George, when you think of life, do you see the glass as half full or half empty?"

"I don't see it as half full or half empty," George replied.

"Then how do you see it?" the biographer asked.

"It is *enough*," George replied. "*Enough.*"

Jimmie loves the book and the philosophy. Jimmie figures if George Dawson, a man who grew up black in one of the toughest times in a country's history for a minority, and a man who was illiterate until 98 could look at life and say, "It is *enough*." If this man could see life as neither half full or half empty, if he could look at life and claim *enough*, then so could he.

For my friend Jimmie, *enough* hasn't just been an attitude, but a lifestyle – and a diet plan. Jimmie travels a lot for work, so he eats out a lot. Eating out usually means an easy road to gaining weight. Jimmie used the power of *enough* to limit what he ate. Instead of eating what he could, or what would make him feel good, he just ate what he needed at each meal. The *Enough* Diet Plan took forty-two pounds off Jimmie even while he was still traveling. *Enough* changed Jimmie's life. It can change yours.

Consider the king in this next story adapted from Heather Forrest's collection *Wisdom Tales*...

Once there was a prince who was so sad, his eyes seemed full of sadness and tears. The king was concerned about his son. He got cooks to prepare the best dishes, toymakers to make the best toys, and teachers to share their most stimulating ideas, but to no avail. No gift or treasure could free the prince from his sadness.

The king called his advisors who offered this solution, "For the prince to be happy, you must dress him in the shirt of a truly happy man. Then he will be cured of all his sorrow."

So the king set out on a journey to find a truly happy man.

He went through the village to the church. The priest always seemed to him to be a happy man. "Your, majesty," the priest said, "to what do I owe this honor?"

The king said, "You are known as a good and holy man. I would like to know, would you accept the position of bishop should it come to you?"

"Certainly," replied the priest.

"Never mind," the king said and left disappointed. If the priest were truly happy, he wouldn't want to be bishop.

The king went to another kingdom and visited another monarch. "My friend," asked the king, "are you happy?"

"Most of the time, but not always, there are many nights I am restless because I am worry about losing all that I have worked so hard to gain."

The king left for he knew that this man's shirt would not do.

On his way back to his own kingdom, he happened to be riding by a farm. He heard singing. He stopped his carriage and followed the sound of the song. There he found a poor farmer, singing at the top of his lungs. The farmer looked up to see the king approaching and said, "Good day, sir!"

"Good day to you," said the king. "You seem so happy today."

"I am happy every day for I am blessed with a wonderful life."

The king said, "Come with me to the castle. You will be surrounded with luxury and never want for anything again."

"Thank you your majesty, but I would not give up my life for all the castles in the world."

The king could not contain his joy. "My son is saved! All I need do is take this man's shirt back to the castle with me!"

It was then the king looked and realized... the man wasn't wearing a shirt.[2]

The king wanted to be happy, and he wanted his son to be happy. Though he searched far and wide, he couldn't find any thing or person that could transform his son from despair to delight, or give peace to his own anxiety. Though sent in search of a shirt, he discovered a secret. Neither he nor his son needed the shirt of a truly happy man. They didn't need a shirt at all. The power wasn't outside the castle or within its walls. The power was, however, in his son and in him. They each had the power to create their own kingdoms of their lives. Power so simple anyone can learn.

Kevin Salwen picked up his fourteen year old daughter, Hannah, from a slumber party and was driving her home. At a red light, Hannah looked out their windows and saw a homeless man on the sidewalk holding up a sign asking for money to buy food. On the other side of the car, in the lane next to them, Hannah saw a black Mercedes.

---

[2] Heather Forest, *Wisdom Tales*, p.117.

She looked from the Mercedes, back to the homeless man, and from the homeless man back again to the Mercedes. Then she said to her father, "If that guy didn't have such a nice car, then that guy could have a nice meal."

It made sense to her. A less expensive car for one man could keep another off the street. Hannah was moved. She challenged her family.

"What do you want to do?" asked Hannah's mother. "Sell our house?"

Her mother was joking. Hannah wasn't. Hannah thought selling the house was a great idea. They could trade their house in for a less expensive one, half the size and half the expense, and donate the difference to charity. And that's what they did.

They contributed half the sale of their house to a non-profit called *The Hunger Project* where the money has gone to impact the lives of thousands in a positive way.

Hannah and her father teamed up to write a book about the project, *The Power of Half*. Hannah told *The New York Times*, "No one expects anyone to sell a house. That's kind of a ridiculous thing to do. For us, the house was just something we could live without. It was too big for us. Everyone has too much of something, whether it's time, talent or treasure. Everyone does have their own half; you just have to find it."

Though some accuse the Salwens of grandstanding, Kevin told *The Times*, "This is the most self-interested thing we have ever done. I'm thrilled that we can help others. I'm blown away by how much it has helped us."

Their charity benefited their family; they gave away wealth and found health; they found addition through subtraction; through the loss of some of their stuff, they gained additional peace of mind; for them, for all of us, that is *enough*.

In your life, like theirs, where do you need to let go of some of your wealth to find health, where have you been caught up in *more, more* and need the power of *enough?*

A simple word.

A powerful word.

Enough.

Say it now.

Enough.

Say it daily.

Enough.

Chapter Two

The Problem

The children of Eden suffered when they wanted something *more*. They lived in paradise, a garden gifted from God, made just for them, yet weren't satisfied. In their search for something more, paradise was lost.

Looking deeper into Eden and the loss of the garden life for insatiable desert, we see how the children of Eden's problems didn't come just because they want something *more*; their problems came when they want something *else*.

The Text

Genesis 3: [6] *So when the woman saw that the tree was good for food, and that it was a delight to the eyes, and that the tree was to be desired to make one wise, she took of its fruit and ate; and she also gave some to her husband, who was with her, and he ate.*

Pretend you are Eve or Adam, looking at the fruit, the appealing fruit, the one you desire. For whatever reason, you see this piece of fruit differently from others, this fruit seems to be the key piece to your life, one fruit better than others, one which fills the incomplete hole in belly and soul, the one preferred above all the rest, forbidden, prohibited, banned, but, for whatever reason, now indispensable, essential, one you cannot do without and be happy, a must have, at all cost, or all is lost.

Now, consider your life, and the lives of those you know. What are your perceived indispensible fruits, your must-haves for happiness?

Does Anthony De Mello describe you in this following quote?

There is only one reason why you're not experiencing bliss at this present moment, and it's because you're thinking or focusing on what you don't have.

Do you focus on what you don't have? Are you in search of some unattained thing, circumstance, relationship on which your happiness depends? Are you incessantly looking for something *else* in which you've put your hope?

The Eden story points us to why our lives may be so unsatisfying. The tree Adam and Eve found so appealing yet so damning was the tree of the knowledge of good and evil. Other translations of the Hebrew words for good and evil here are helpful for a clearer understanding of the tree in the story and of our suffering. The tree of the knowledge of *good and evil* may be translated as: the knowledge of *good and bad, good and not so good,* or of *good and less-than.*

This dualistic, dividing, labeling, classifying knowledge is often what we seek.

Think of how frequently you discern between good and bad, or good and less-than. Walk through any grocery store, on a single aisle, how many times do you rate items from the good to the not so good or bad?

Think of people you know. How often do you rank a person's behavior as good or not so good, or the persons themselves?

Think of life experiences. How often do you rate your life experiences?

Think about the experiences in the following list. Which do you think is better?

Being rich or being poor?
Being married or being single?
Being healthy or being ill?
Having children or not having children?
Having a job or being unemployed?
Being younger or being older?
Living or dying?

Were those questions difficult for you? Probably not.

Our general, often unspoken, consensus is that being rich is better than being poor, being married is better than being single, being healthy is better than being ill, having children is better than not having children, having a job is better than not having a job, being younger is better than being older, and living is better than dying.

This judging, this preferring one over another, this quest to know the good from the not so good, or the good from the less-than, could have been the source of the suffering for Adam and Eve in the Eden story, and it can be that same labeling is the source for our suffering.

Jianzhi Sengcan (d. 606) wrote that it is our attempts to discern good from less-than which causes us to suffer. And our liberation from our suffering, our key to a happy fulfilled life, comes from doing away with preferences. Sengcan wrote,

The Great Way is not difficult
for those who have no preferences.
When love and hate (like and dislike) are both absent
everything becomes clear and undisguised.

Make the smallest distinction, however,
and heaven and earth are set infinitely apart.
If you wish to see the truth
then hold no opinions for or against anything.

To set up what you like against what you dislike
is the disease of the mind.
When the deep meaning of things is not understood
the mind's essential (stillness) is disturbed to no avail.[3]

If you're like me, when you read *have no preferences...* you think, 'What do you mean, 'have no preferences? How can you not like being rich over being poor? being healthy over being ill? being in a relationship to being alone? being employed to unemployed? being alive over dead? That's crazy! After all, isn't being well better than being ill, being in relationship better than being out,

---

[3] Jianzhi Sengcan (d. 606), *Hsin Shin Ming,* or *Trust in Mind,* this translation from the book *Trust in Mind* by Mu Soeng.

being rich better than being poor, being alive better than being dead?'

Well, is it? In the world as you observe it, are riches, health, or relationship any guarantee of happiness? Are healthy people necessarily happier than sick? Are rich people necessarily happier than poor? There are plenty of people with money who are unhappy, plenty of physically healthy people who are chronically sad, and, there are terminally ill people who are happy, divorced people who are satisfied, and unemployed people who are content. The difference is not their circumstances.

In Eden, isn't it as soon as they pursue the forbidden fruit as their something *more*, their something *else*, as their *if only...*, that paradise is lost? Isn't it true with us, as soon as we pursue something *else*, convinced that our lives short of this next desire are deficient, that we begin to suffer?

Consider these following people. Will their *if only* thinking lead them to or away from happiness?

The single person: *If only I was married, then I'd be happy.*

The married person: *If only I had kids, then I'd be happy.*

The parent: *If only my children respected me, then I'd be happy.*

The unemployed person: *If only I had a job, then I'd be happy.*

The employed person: *If only I got paid more, then I'd be happy.*

The sick person: *If only I were healthy, then I'd be happy.*

The adult: *If only I was younger, then I'd be happy.*

The child: *If only I was older, then I'd be happy.*

All of these assume, *if only I had something else then I would be happy.* Are they right? Of course not. After all, if marriage was the end all to happiness, would there be so many divorces? If parenting brought nothing but joy, would there be so much abuse and neglect? If employment or pay gave us happiness would so many people leave their jobs for another?

If only leads us to the mistake of Adam and Eve, thinking that our happiness results from that one more piece of fruit. If happiness was something gained outside ourselves, through some formulated circumstance, then with all the change over the past two hundred years, wouldn't we be the happiest people on earth? If *more* brought happiness, wouldn't we be the happiest people who ever lived?

Consider our advances. Over the past two centuries, statesmen and political leaders have broadened the ability of government to shape communities for the better. Scientists have developed theories that set the foundation for industry after industry. Engineers in large companies have designed tools, machines, vehicles, electronics and appliances that have altered our daily lives. Professors and researchers have written books upon books about how our minds work and how we behave socially. Psychologists have developed therapies, and doctors have developed medicine and treatments to make us healthier. Yet, with all these advancements, with so much *more* than any generation of people has ever had before in the history of humanity, there is no evidence that we are happier today than people were a hundred or a thousand years ago.

We still think there is something *more*, something *else* in order to be happy, one more *if only...* which if we could get it, would make us happy. So we search our gardens, looking for the preferred thing, person, or experience, and like Adam and Eve, our hope for living in paradise is lost.

We know their story, but we keep chasing after the next apple, even though the next apple won't make us content, finally once and for all happy.   The reality is no fruit, experience, or situation will make an unhappy person happy. Studies of past lottery winners show that people who were happy before winning the lottery are happy after winning the lottery, and people who were unhappy before winning the lottery are unhappy after winning the lottery.

It is not the piece of fruit, the lottery ticket, the job, the spouse, or any other desirable that will give us satisfaction or contentment. Those must begin within, not changing the world but our orientation toward the world.

What we need is something Adam and Eve didn't know. We need *enough*, and we need another word, another word to help us find happiness regardless of our circumstances, another word to help us find contentment even in the midst of great challenges, another to help us not only live differently but be differently. We need a word like...

Ahhh

The Text Revisited

What if Adam and Eve had known *Ahhh* as well as *Enough*? If they had, their story would have likely gone something like this...

Genesis 3: *the woman saw that the tree was good for food, and that it was a delight to the eyes, and that the tree was to be desired to make one wise...* but then she said to herself, "What are you thinking? You live in a beautiful garden. This is paradise. You have everything you need to be happy right here. You have *enough*." She said it to herself again, "*Enough*." Adam, who was with her affirmed, "Yes, we have *enough*."

She thought, "Lots of trees here have good fruit just like that one. There's no reason to think I'd be any fuller or happier with fruit from this tree." She looked at the piece of fruit in her hand, a piece of fruit she had picked earlier from another tree. She took a bite from it and said, *Ahhh*. She gave some to her husband. He took a bite and said, *Ahhh*.

Then the two walked on, together.

Transformation

There once was a king who was so worried that he couldn't sleep at night. He was worried, not because things were going badly in his kingdom, but because things were going well. Things had been going so well since he took his father's throne, so well that he knew they couldn't go that well for long. So he worried.

One evening, as he sat on his throne, the young prince of four years old sitting beside him, he called his advisors before him.

"Sages, I am troubled as king. I am worried for the future and I need your help. The one of you that gives me the best advice will receive this as his reward." In the kings hand he held a very precious jewel. "What I want to know is, what is the most important thing for me to do as king, and when should I do it?"

Advisor after advisor came, with suggestions on planning, diet, exercise... none seemed to answer the king's question of what he should do and when he should do it.

The king became bored, but not as bored as the young prince sitting next to him. The young prince rocked in his chair. He tottered then fell over backward. He wasn't hurt but he was stuck underneath his chair and couldn't get up. The king was so busy thinking about the future of the kingdom that he didn't notice his young son fall over.

"Father..." the boy cried out.

"Not now my son, I'm listening to my advisors...sort of..."

"Father, I need you..."

"Not now..."

"Father, I need you now!"

The king looked over to his son, seeing his imprisonment he got up from his throne and turned over the chair and rescued his son. "You did need me now, didn't you?" the king asked, and there was his answer.

"Thank you, my sages," he said to his advisors, "I appreciate your help. But the best answer came today from my son." Then he handed the prince the jewel. "The best thing for me to do as king is act, the best time to act is always now, for now is all that I have."

He called for his son. Took him into his arms. He held him tight. He laughed. "I love being with you," he said. Then, so soft only his son could hear it, he said, "Ahhh..."[4]

In moments other than now, we cannot be content. Contentment comes now. The king in the previous story learned that peace is only found in the present, no matter what good advice he got for the future, he could only say *Ahhh* in the present.

Hinduism offers a sound, *Om*. This sound is said to connect us to God, a form of prayer. I haven't had much success praying *Om*. However, I have found *Ahhh* to be quite helpful.

For Adam and Eve in the garden, their quest for something more, something else, distanced them from God, I wonder if *Ahhh* would have helped them see just how close God was. It does for me. *Ahhh* relaxes me, opens my heart and mind, and creates in me a sense of peace. Joseph Wood Krutch, American naturalist, said, "Happiness is itself a kind of gratitude." I find in *Ahhh* a sound, a prayer of gratitude, thanking God for the present moment, the present life, the present breath.

Consider your life.

Consider this moment right now.

Concentrate on your breathing.

Feel your chest and stomach move with each breath.

Open wide and say, *Ahhh.*

Say it again, *Ahhh.*

Once more, *Ahhh.*

---

[4] I searched for the source of this story and couldn't find it. I'm not sure if I read it or heard it, but to the unnamed author, please accept my apology for not crediting you and my gratitude for a wonderful story, one essential to this chapter.

Chapter Three

I've got it bad and that ain't good.
Etta James

The Problem

Between a long hallway and the playground of our church used to be an old door with plate glass windows in it. My son showed us just how dangerous those old windows can be.

Nathan, age seven, and a friend were running down the hallway to go back outside after a trip to the bathroom.

The two were racing.

The door was locked.

Nathan got to the door first, pushed hard, trying not to slow down.

The door didn't move. His hand went through the window. He ran for help.

Applying pressure, afraid he had severed an artery, we called an ambulance. We went to Vanderbilt Children's Hospital where Nate received, among other things, eighteen stitches.

In the days following, I struggled with how to talk about Nathan's accident and what language to use. His wound was *really bad*, but not *really, really bad*. It was *really bad* that the cut was so deep, but not *really, really bad* because he didn't sever the tendon. It was *bad* that he cut his arm, but *good* that he didn't cut an artery.

Nathan said often, "I wish this didn't happen." We agreed. If given the choice, we would rather it didn't happen, but we were glad, since it happened, he wasn't hurt worse. So we said to him, "Son, we're sad it happened too, but we're glad it wasn't worse. It was bad it happened but good it wasn't badder, we mean worse."

Nathan looked at us and said, "Huh?"

I have to concur. When I hear myself, and others, speak of situations and circumstances, experiences and outcomes, using the language of *good* and *bad* labeling, then I, like Nathan, often reply, "Huh?"

Labeling *good* and *bad* on our experiences is difficult, complex, and even more so once it becomes theological. We add the God question, "Where was God? Where was God when Nathan shoved his hand through the window?"

When things happen which we perceive as good, people of faith often say we are *blessed* meaning that God is watching kindly over us. But what about when we suffer pain like with Nathan's accident? Where was God? Would we say God was watching out for him that he didn't do more damage, or God wasn't watching out for him that he had to have 18 stitches? Were we blessed that he didn't do more damage or were we cursed that he did any damage at all?

Nearby our home at the writing of this chapter, many residents in Murfreesboro (forty miles away) were hit by tornadoes. We struggled with what language to use. We weren't the only ones. I saw a minister interviewed on television. The people from his church were doing a lot for those who lost their homes or experienced great damage from the tornadoes.

He was asked, "Was your home hit?"

"No," he said, "praise God."

I wondered, "Is that it? Praise God for looking out for our homes, but you and yours... well... sorry."

The thinking was clear to me, "Those who weren't hit... we're blessed." But the converse was left unspoken, "Those who were hit... are cursed." Clearly, we think, "Homes not hit by tornado... *that's good*. And homes hit by tornado... *that's bad*." But how God is involved is not so apparent. I have two masters degrees, twenty years of full time church ministry, and I often struggle with good and bad and God.

The struggle with good, bad, and God isn't a new struggle for me, though, when younger, it was funny. When I was a Boy Scout, we told a campfire story that illustrates how tough labeling experiences good and bad can be. Read it with me. Your lines are in *italics*.

A pilot went up for a solo flight in his airplane. Before he left, he made sure the airplane was in good condition and everything was in working order.

That's good.

But there was a kink in the motor's design which the pilot couldn't see, and the motor gave out.

That's bad.

He decided to abandon the plane and found a parachute.

That's good.

He jumped out of the plane but the parachute wouldn't open.

That's bad.

There was a haystack.

That's good.

He headed, as best he could, toward the haystack, and then saw a pitchfork pointed up in the haystack.

That's bad.
He missed the pitchfork.
That's good.
But he also missed the haystack...
Oh,...
Yeah, oh....

Consider also this story. Again, your lines are in *italics...*

A friend was driving to his church in Michigan in January...
That's good. Going to church is good.
But the roads were icy, his car slid and he crashed into a tree.
That was bad.
Along came another member of the church.
That's good.
But he slid on the same spot and crashed into the man's car.
That's bad.
But then came a policeman.
That's good.
But he slid into the cars and crashed into them and my friend got injured.
That's bad.
The ambulance came, after it crashed into the cars it took my friend to the hospital.
That's good.
But they said his leg was broken, and my friend would have to have surgery.
That's bad.
But he fell in love with his nurse...

Well, that's good.

And when he got out of the hospital, they flew to Vegas and got married.

That's good.

(Pause.)

That's good, isn't it?

Maybe... yesterday, she, her six kids, two dogs, three cats, a gold fish, and a gerbil moved into his two bedroom apartment.

Oh...

Yeah, oh...

Determining what's good and bad can be a twisting and turning ride, in an instant, what you thought good now seems bad and what you thought bad suddenly seems good.

With labeling experiences good or bad being so difficult, a rational mind might conclude that we would attempt such classifications less, but not so, not for me. No matter how hard, no matter how incompetent I am at it, I want to label things, experiences, and people as *good* or *bad*. I want in all confidence to boldly say, "This was *good*." "This was *bad*." So, I tag frequently and often.

I label meals. "How was dinner?" "It was good." I label worship. "How was worship? The music was wonderful, but the sermon was bad." I label things I do. "Carrie," I say, "I did something bad." "What did you do?" she asks. "I backed into the mailbox and dented the bumper." Fender benders are bad.

I label not only experiences but whole days. "How was your day?" Carrie will ask. I'll sum up the whole day's experiences as either "I had a good day," or "I had a bad day." Ask me about the weather? "How's the weather out there?" "Great!" or "Nasty!" I can sum up whole years as good or bad. Ask me, "How is life at the church?" I'll likely tell you, "It's been a good year," or "It's been a challenging (bad) year."

I label my children's behavior, "Why can't you be good?" "What are you acting so badly?" In my world, labels abound.

It seems my quest to sort through life labeling experiences, days, weeks, months, behaviors, and events as good or bad. My quest seems common. I know others who label as I do. It gives us something to talk about, rejoice about, or complain about. If you meet someone and don't know what to talk about, find a common dislike and you can talk for hours on how bad the schools are, the government, the coffee at church, the coach of the local sports team... on and on...

Labeling is a common trait of humanity. We label, tag, brand, classify, pigeonhole, and catalog. We name good or bad frequently and often. Apparently, we have for a long, long time. Consider the age old story of Adam and Eve.

Adam and Eve are walking along when they come across a snake at the tree of knowledge, "Step right up," the snake says. "What we have here is a nice piece of fruit that will give you what you're looking for. One bite and you'll no longer worry about what's good or what's bad, you'll know. You'll have the God-like knowledge to give you the power to know good from evil, good from bad... Say, you look like a fine couple... how would you like to have the power that can change your life?"

That's what we want. God-like power to be able to label things as good and bad. "Give us that knowledge! Give it to us now!"

But God won't. Consider Jesus. If you are looking to Jesus for the power to label your life's components as *good* or *bad* then watch out. He won't do it. When you look for certainty, Jesus is like a guy who says to you, "You want a safe spot? Come stand out here in the middle of the room. Come stand in the middle on this carpet. Feel safe, yet? You do? Good." Then he'll pull the rug right out from under you.

Consider his life. Labeling good and bad is extremely problematic.

Jesus comes into Jerusalem and the crowds are all for him screaming Hosanna!

That's good. People are cheering for him. They seem to get it.

But the leaders of the day don't like it, and the Roman authorities are nervous.

That's bad.

Jesus gets away, and goes to a safe place. And the leaders don't know where to find him.

That's good. Jesus is safe. Safe is good.

But one of his followers has betrayed him.

That's bad. Betrayal by someone you love is always bad.

But Jesus knows about it ahead of time.

That's good. Jesus had choices. Choices are good.

But Jesus washes his soon-to-be-betrayer's feet, gives him something to eat, and then lets him go.

That's nice, but that's bad. Send the traitor away. Go somewhere else and hide.

Even after the betrayer leaves, Jesus still has time to get away.

That's good.

But he doesn't go away. Instead, he goes to a nearby garden and prays while waiting for those who will do him harm.

That's bad. Why wait when you can hide?

Some of Jesus' followers resist.

That's good. Jesus' followers love him. They are willing to fight for him.

But Jesus tells them not to.

Again, that's nice, but that's also bad.

They accuse Jesus, beat him, make him carry his own cross, and crucify him.

That's terrible.

Yes, that's terrible, horrible, one of the worst things we can imagine, and that is on the day we call *Good* Friday.

Good Friday? On the day Jesus was brutally killed, suffered torture before he died, abandoned by the authorities and his closest friends and followers, do we have any idea what we are talking about when we call it *Good* Friday? Perhaps not.

Perhaps in all our labeling of *good* and *bad* we have no idea what we are talking about.

Perhaps that's the point.

The Text

On the Sunday following *Good* Friday, the women went to the tomb where Jesus was buried.

To them, there was nothing *good* about the previous Friday. They saw only *bad* with nothing *good* ahead.

Mark 16: *When the Sabbath was over, Mary Magdalene, and Mary the mother of James, and Salome bought spices, so that they might go and anoint him. ² And very early on the first day of the week, when the sun had risen, they went to the tomb. ³ They had been saying to one another, "Who will roll away the stone for us from the entrance to the tomb?"*

Walking to the tomb, wanting to care for the body of Jesus, their loved one, certain a boulder would be blocking their way, feeling as powerless to care for his body as they had felt when they wanted to keep him from being crucified, they saw only *bad* ahead, no *good* was possible.

Then they get to the tomb, and beyond imagination, beyond possibility, the stone is moved and no soldiers but an angel.

⁴ *When they looked up, they saw that the stone, which was very large, had already been rolled back. ⁵ As they entered the tomb, they saw a young man, dressed in a white robe, sitting on the right side; and they were alarmed. ⁶ But he said to them, "Do not be alarmed; you are looking for Jesus of Nazareth, who was crucified. He has been raised; he is not here. Look, there is the place they laid him. ⁷ But go, tell his disciples and Peter that he is going ahead of you to Galilee; there you will see him, just as he told you."*

So what did they do after they heard the contradicting angel saying joyously that what they saw as impossibly bad was actually a great day?

[8] *So they went out and fled from the tomb, for terror and amazement had seized them; and they said nothing to anyone, for they were afraid.*

They ran and hid.

If we had been there, and heard the angel, what do you think we would have done? Chances are we would have done what the women in the story did, run away and hide. That's what we do. We label *good* and *bad*, and if we can't figure it out, if it doesn't meet our labels, we'll run from it, and Jesus is no help. With Jesus, you can't count on the *bad* being *bad*, nor can you count on the *bad* being final. Jesus was dead. That's bad. Surely that's bad. But then he, according to the angel, was walking around alive, setting up appointments, meeting with people. Jesus, once dead, was alive. It was too much for the women, and us, to imagine.

At the tomb, the women came in afraid and left afraid, they came in grief and left in grief, they came in pain and left in pain. They weren't ready for anything else.

The women had *good*, they had *bad*. To experience a miracle on Easter, they needed another word, a magic word, something more than *good* or *bad* alone can give. They needed...

Maybe

The Text Revisited

If the women on the way to the tomb had known about *maybe*, then they could have experienced and rejoiced in the Easter miracle. Consider what might have happened in this retelling...

Mark 16: *When the sabbath was over, Mary Magdalene, and Mary the mother of James, and Salome bought spices, so that they might go and anoint him.* [2] *And very early on the first day of the week, when the sun had risen, they went to the tomb.* [3] *They had been saying to one another, "Who will roll away the stone for us from the entrance to the tomb?"*... And they thought, "All our dreams died with Jesus. Now we are going to finish burying the one we not only followed but loved. That large rock is so big that we'll never get it moved on our own. This *may be* one of the best days of our lives!"

Maybe would have allowed them to be present, really present, on Easter instead of blinded by their fear. *Maybe* would have opened a door of possibility.

If the ones who went to the tomb on Easter had remembered the first chapter from Genesis, they could have saved themselves the trouble. In the first chapter of Genesis, God creates by saying, "Let there be light," then, God names, "God called the light, Day..." and then God discerns, "God saw that it was *good*." God is the one who discerns what is *good*, not humanity. *Good* is left up to God.

The women were certain they had the knowledge of what was *good* and what wasn't. They were certain both Friday and Sunday qualified as *bad* and only *bad* days.

They didn't see that like Genesis chapter one, God gets the final word on what is *good* or not. They didn't see that any situation where any circumstance where God is at work, any predicament, might be *good*.

They needed *maybe*. They didn't have it, but we can. We certainly need it.

Theology, for centuries, has wrestled with one question over and over again without resolution. Theologians call it the Theodicy problem: how can God be good when bad things happen?

Maybe asserts that our assumption is wrong about *bad* things in the world. *Maybe* asserts that when it comes to *good* and *bad*, we can never be quite sure. *Maybe* asserts that in this uncertainty is possibility, for even in the most painful and challenging parts of our lives, wonders may abound. So at any particular moment, we can't know for sure *good* or *bad* because our sight and understanding are both limited.

So, the healthier approach to *good* and *bad* is the simple, *maybe*. Consider the farmer in the following story...

Transformation

A farmer lived with his family on a small farm. They were not rich for it was not a large farm. They had a small barn and a good horse they used to plow the fields and ride to town when the occasion arose.

One day, the horse ran away. Then the farmer's neighbors came by and said, "O' no! You lost your horse. That's bad." The farmer replied, "Maybe. I don't know if it is good or bad. Only God can say."

A week later, the farmer's horse returned but it wasn't alone. The horse returned with a wild stallion accompanying it. The farmer took both horses and placed them in the corral. The same neighbors came by and said, "Wow, you have two horses. That's good!"

The farmer replied, "Maybe. I don't know if it is good or bad. Only God can say."

A few days later, the farmer's son was trying to tame the new horse. The stallion threw the son off its back. When the son hit the ground he broke his hip. Though he healed, he never was quite the same and walked with a limp. Again the neighbors came by. "Oh, your son broke his hip, that's bad."

The farmer replied, "Maybe. I don't know if it is good or bad. Only God can say."

A year later, the army came through the nearby village. The army was short on troops so they took every young and able man of the village and surrounding area with them. When they came by the farm, they did not take the farmer's son since he still traveled slowly with his limp. The neighbors came by and said, "The army didn't take your son. Isn't that good?"

The farmer replied, "Maybe. Only God can say." He paused for a moment and whispered, "But I think it's pretty good."

After Jesus died, the disciples were without hope. Caught up in the tragedy of Jesus' death, they had *bad* and only *bad*. All they could see was the tragic end and nothing more. Yet, if they had *maybe* in their vocabulary, then their experience of Easter would have been different. If they had *maybe*, they could have gone to the tomb, women and men, with an expectant hope, with minds open to what might be.

"Jesus died? that's terrible!" *Maybe.*

"Soldiers came for Jesus. They may come for you." That's bad. *Maybe.*

"Jesus' body is in the tomb. There's a rock in front of it." It's over. This is final. *Maybe.*

Easter opens every experience to the potential of God at work. What's true for Jesus is true for us, whatever injustice, whatever evil, whatever tragedy befalls us, good may come from them all, why? Because God says so. Is it good or bad? *Maybe. Only God can say.* That's the good news of Easter: any bad can be the setting stage for God at work, any trial *may be* good unseen.

So, when my son shoved his arm through a window and cut himself, was it bad? *Maybe.* It sure was painful, but whether or not it was bad is something only God can say.

When the tornadoes hit some houses, was it bad? *Maybe.* It certainly was frightening, frustrating, and for a few, fatal, but whether or not it was bad is something only God can say.

The gospel story points us to a new reality, a reality beyond simple, fatal, determined *good* and *bad.* The gospel story points us to an open, potential, possible reality where even death is not final, where crosses become signs of hope, where tombs become doorways, and where ends become possibilities for new beginnings.

The angel's message of Easter is that anywhere and everywhere has the working potential of God at play where every outcome is uncertain, and where labels of *good* and *bad*, *life* and *death*, *helpless* or *hopeless*, are futile. Once a dead guy gets out of a tomb and starts walking around, uncertainties abound, and *maybes* are everywhere. For with God, any situation, no matter how terrible or terrifying *may become* wonderful.

The angel has come. Do you hear him? Today may be the best day of your life. Today may be the day when some pain, some abuse, or some tragedy clearly becomes a doorway to new life and new possibility. Isn't it time you gave it a *maybe*?

Chapter Four

Oh, No, No, No...
Bruce Springsteen

The Problem

Amen.

I am told that *amen* means *so be it*. *So be it* is a lot like *yes*. When I imagine Adam walking through Eden, I imagine him saying, "Yes," a lot.

God says, "Adam, work the garden."

Adam says, "Yes," and works the garden.

God says, "Adam, name the animals."

Adam says, "Yes," and names the animals.

God says, "Adam, enjoy the garden."

Adam says, "Yes," and enjoys the beauty of the garden.

I imagine Adam walking through the marvels of Eden, the wonders upon wonders, the joys, the sights, and the vistas which, upon seeing, Adam says from deep in his soul, "Yes! Yes! Yes!"

Wendell Berry captures for me what first wonders feel like in his poem, *The First*.

> *The first man who whistled*
> *thought he had a wren in his mouth.*
> *He went around all day*
> *with his lips puckered,*
> *afraid to swallow.*

Yes. Yes. Yes.

Adam knew *yes*.

He also knew *no*.

God says, "Adam don't eat from the tree that is in the middle of the garden."

Adam says, "Which tree?" And later, when he's sure God is far away, when he holds the fruit in his hand, Adam says, "No," and breaks God's rule.

When God looks for him, when God asks what he has done, Adam doesn't say *yes* to God but *no*. "No! It wasn't my fault. It was that woman you gave me." *No*.

Adam had *yes*. Adam had *no*. He needed something else.

Peter, Jesus' disciple, was a lot like Adam. Peter had *yes*. Peter had *no*. He needed something else.

The Text

Mark 8: *²⁷ Jesus went on with his disciples to the villages of Caesarea Philippi; and on the way he asked his disciples, "Who do people say that I am?" ²⁸ And they answered him, "John the Baptist; and others, Elijah; and still others, one of the prophets." ²⁹ He asked them, "But who do you say that I am?" Peter answered him, "You are the Messiah." ³⁰ And he sternly ordered them not to tell anyone about him.*

³¹ Then he began to teach them that the Son of Man must undergo great suffering, and be rejected by the elders, the chief priests, and the scribes, and be killed, and after three days rise again. ³² He said all this quite openly. And Peter took him aside and began to rebuke him. ³³ But turning and looking at his disciples, he rebuked Peter and said, "Get behind me,

Satan! For you are setting your mind not on divine things but on human things."

Peter was big on saying, "Yes!"

Jesus found Peter on the shores of Galilee. Jesus said, "Come and follow me."

Peter responded, "Yes!"

Jesus was walking on water. Jesus said, "Come to me."

Peter said, "Yes!" and stepped out of the boat.

Jesus said, "Feed the 5,000 people with five loaves and two fish."

And Peter said, "Yes!"

Jesus said, "We're riding into Jerusalem."

Peter got excited and said, "YES!"

Jesus started throwing the money changers out of the temple. Peter even more excited shouted, "YES! YES! YES!"

But Peter didn't just say, "Yes," to Jesus. When Jesus talked about his death, "They will kill me in Jerusalem," when Jesus tried to prepare him, Peter wouldn't hear of it. He couldn't say, "Yes," to the death of Jesus whom he loved so much, so Peter shouted, "NO!" He said, "No, Jesus, that can never happen to you! NO!"

When they came for Jesus, Peter took his sword and cut off the ear of another man. "NO! You can't take him!" But they did.

Peter, afraid that they might take him away like they took Jesus, and crucify him like they were about to crucify Jesus, accused of knowing Jesus, of being one of Jesus' followers, Peter shouted, "NO! I don't know him!" Three times he shouted, "NO! NO! NO!"

Peter understood *yes*. Peter understood *no*. He needed something else. If he had only had something else, Peter might have been able to stay with Jesus, to have been present when Jesus had needed him. If only Peter had something more. But he didn't. He had *yes*. He had *no*. But nothing else.

I was like Adam. I was like Peter. I had *yes*. I had *no*. But I needed something else, especially when my father was dying.

I was 18 years old, starting my sophomore year in college, my father was in the hospital. He was dying of cancer, and I didn't know it. I had *yes* and I had *no* but I didn't have anything else.

I had *yes* you are going to get better, *yes* you'll be going back home from the hospital, *yes* it won't be long now.

I also had *no*. *No*, the doctor didn't really say it could be any time. *No* he's not looking worse by the moment. *No...*

My father was dying, but I couldn't see it. I couldn't be present with him. I had *yes*. I had *no*. I needed something else.

When I went to the hospital that Friday night, my mother had been with him for several days, so I volunteered to sit by his bed so she could sleep.

All men may be created equal (according to the Declaration of Independence) but all nurses definitely are not. My father's night nurse was named Attila. She jabbed my father more times putting in his i.v. than Attila the Hun jabbed Asia. I sat beside his bed. He kept sitting up. His eyes glazed, he reached up and beyond the wall of the room. I didn't know that he was dying. All I knew was that he was pulling out his i.v. I knew I didn't want Attila to come back and jab him anymore. I kept saying, "No..." "No, Dad..." "No, Dad, lie back..." I didn't know he was dying.

My consistent, "No," kept him in the hospital room through the night.

After the sun came up and mom woke up, I went to the house for a shower. About a half hour after I left, with my resistance out of the room, with my *no* out of his way, he died.

My family wanted to tell me in person, when they got home, so they waited. At home, alone, I answered the phone. The man from the funeral home spoke to me looking for mom. "Did you know Mr. Jones died?" he asked. All I could say was, "No..."

That was some twenty-five plus years ago. During the writing of this chapter, I got another phone call. A young man in our community committed suicide. His father came home and found him. He had hung himself in the garage.

When I got the news, all I could say was, "No..."

Shep was a vibrant young man, active across several groups, football player, skateboarder, Young Life active participant. Shep said *yes* to much of life, to friends, to school, to God. Shep also said *no*. When he took his life, Shep cried a loud, incomprehensible and irreversible, "NO!"

Shep had *yes*. Shep had *no*. Shep needed something else.

Jesus had something else. Jesus knew a word Adam didn't know. Jesus knew a word Peter didn't know. Jesus knew a word I didn't know. Jesus knew a word that Shep didn't know. Jesus knew a word we needed. Jesus knew a word all of us need...

Okay

The Text Revisited

Imagine if, along with *yes* and *no*, Peter had *okay*...

Mark 8: [31] *Then (Jesus) began to teach them that the Son of Man must undergo great suffering, and be rejected by the elders, the chief priests, and the scribes, and be killed, and after three days rise again.* [32] *He said all this quite openly.* And Peter said, *"Okay. I don't like it, but okay..."*

Transformation

Jesus knew *okay*.

In the Garden of Gethsemane, soldiers were coming for Jesus. Jesus knew the people in power would rather have him dead than alive, and they had the ability to end his life. Jesus looked to God, prayed three times, but as far as we know, God, who spoke to him at his baptism and called him beloved, said nothing here. Jesus prayed again and again, "My Father, if it is possible, let this cup pass from me; yet not what I want but what you want."

if it is possible... When it came to Jesus' own death, not everything was clear. He looked for other possibilities, possibilities that were out of sight for him...

let this cup pass from me... He wanted another way. This wasn't his first choice, so he didn't shout, "YES!" like a high school cheerleader at homecoming, like a couple who has been given the news that their in vitro succeeded, like a man who just won the lottery and is told to go to the store of purchase to claim his winnings, no, nothing like that. No alternatives were given that would keep Jesus from the painful road ahead. Death was imminent. And so Jesus, although he doesn't give a certain, "Yes," he does answer in the affirmative. He says, essentially, "Okay." "If this is your will, your plan, then, okay."

Amen means *so be it. So be it* doesn't always sound like *yes* to me. Often it sounds more like *okay.* Sometimes, we don't have a *yes* to give. Sometimes, like Adam in the Garden when he'd blown it, like when Peter faced the death of one he loved, like me with the death of my father, and all of us in our troubles, sometimes *okay* is all we can muster.

But even if it is all we can find in affirmation, *okay* is plenty, a holy *amen* in the presence of God.

Consider: If Adam had known *okay,* then things likely would have been different in his story. If when God said, "Don't eat from that tree," he had said, "Okay," he would have saved himself a lot of trouble.

Similarly, with Peter, if when Jesus said, "Peter I see how this thing is going to turn out, I am going to be killed," and Peter could have said, "Okay," he could have stayed with Jesus, been present with him on his journey to Jerusalem, to the cross, and beyond. If he could have said, "Okay, here we are," when Jesus said to the soldiers, "Okay, here I am," then Peter could have stayed with Jesus.

If I had known *okay* I could have been present with the reality of my father's encroaching death and been present with my father.

If Shep had only known *okay* he could have lived to be with us another day, today.

Okay is a powerful word.

Lao Tzu understood *okay* when he wrote this famous passage in *The Tao*...

> *At birth all people are soft and yielding.*
> *At death they are hard and stiff.*
> *All green plants are tender and yielding.*
> *At death they are brittle and dry.*
> *When hard and rigid,*
> *We consort with death.*
> *When soft and flexible,*
> *We affirm greater life.*

Adam and Eve were hard and stiff. Peter was hard and stiff. I was hard and stiff. But I've learned a lot since then. I've learned that a key word of faith is *okay*. One of the primary things I do now as a pastor is help people find *okay*.

There were two deaths within our community at the same time I was writing this chapter. One was Shep. The other was Joe. Joe understood what Shep didn't. Joe had *yes*. Joe had *no*. Joe also understood *okay*.

I sat with Joe Griswold, church member, husband, father, grandfather, friend, Marine (once a Marine always a Marine, so I'm told). Joe was dying of pancreatic cancer. Pancreatic cancer, according to Joe, was like hearing a gun shot and waiting for the bullet.

I asked, "Joe, remind me what *Semper Fi* (the Marine motto) means."

"Always faithful," Joe replied. "*Fi* is from the Latin *Fides*, or faithful. Always faithful."

For Joe, as for many Marines, *Semper Fi* wasn't a motto, but a lifestyle.

One of Joe's early jobs was with the Post Office. Though they didn't use the Latin, *Semper Fi*, their motto was essentially, always faithful, no matter what the circumstances. *Neither rain, nor snow, nor sleet, nor hail shall keep the postmen from their appointed rounds.* The motto for curriers goes back way before the modern post office, 2,000 years or more. The original saying was actually, *Neither snow, nor rain, nor heat, nor gloom of night stays these courageous couriers from the swift completion of their appointed rounds*

As a Marine, Joe fought in Korea, in the Chosin Reservoir, where the U.N. forces were outnumbered 10 to 1. The weather was so cold the temperature would likely kill you before the enemy could, so cold an injured man would likely watch his own blood freeze, so cold the food, even if you could thaw it, couldn't be cooked enough to not make you sick. *Semper Fi* in Korea meant always faithful regardless of conditions.

As an engineer, Joe worked on The New River Bridge in West Virginia. The New River Bridge is the second tallest bridge in the United States and the longest spanning, steel, single-arch bridge in the world soaring 876 feet above the rugged whitewaters of West Virginia's New River. Because of the bridge, a once 40 minute trip across the river now only takes a single minute. Like any bridge, the sign of a good bridge is *Semper Fi*, always faithful, and the sign of a great bridge, always faithful no matter what the circumstances.

As a church member, always faithful no matter what the circumstances took a different meaning. There were some things about church Joe didn't like. Once a year we have "African Drum Sunday" when almost all the music is accompanied by a drum corp. Joe didn't like the drums. A few times a year, we do Communion by intinction (when people come to the front and tear a piece of bread and dip into the cup instead of passing bread and juice on trays). Joe didn't like it. I know each piece in our worship services Joe didn't like, but Joe never even thought of leaving the church because of any one of those things.

In his marriage of fifty years, *always faithful* was more than a motto, for Joe and Katherine, *always faithful* was a lifestyle.

As we sat together at the hospital, I asked Joe, "What did you learn from your time in the military that has helped you deal with pancreatic cancer and what's going on in your body?"

Joe thought for a minute and said, "Shit happens."

I said to Joe, "It's not personal?"

Joe replied, "I don't think so. Do you?"

"No," I replied.

We sat for a while longer, and then Joe said. "The other thing I learned from the military is you never know what's next."

"But you keep going forward," I said.

"Yes, you keep going forward," he agreed.

I explained to him the *yes, no,* and *okay* distinctions I was working on. He explained to me that *okay* is going forward when you don't know what's next, you don't know what's coming, you don't like it, you may be afraid of it, but you keep going forward. That's *okay*.

Joe's faith allowed him to say *okay* in life and death.

Katherine asked Joe what he thought heaven would be like. Joe said, "Many mansions."

"How can you be so sure?" Katherine asked.

"Because my grandmother told me so," Joe said.

"Do you have any other images?" Katherine asked.

"No," Joe said. He needed none. What his grandmother told him was enough.

The image of mansions is from John 14:

¹Let not your heart be troubled: ye believe in God, believe also in me. ²In my Father's house are many mansions: if it were not so, I would have told you. I go to prepare a place for you. ³And if I go and prepare a place for you, I will come again, and receive you unto myself; that where I am, there ye may be also. (KJV)

In this passage, it is a bridegroom and bride image. A groom in Jesus' day wasn't likely living in his own home or renting an apartment, but in his father's house. In John 14, Jesus speaks as a groom when he says, "In my father's house, there are many dwelling places" in other words, lots of room for rooms.

The groom would begin the engagement, not by proposing to the bride, but to her father. They would negotiate a price, a dowry, for the bride.

Paul also uses language of bride and bridegroom in 1 Corinthians 6:

Do you not know that your body is a temple of the Holy Spirit within you, which you have from God, and that you are not your own? ²⁰ For you were bought with a price; therefore glorify God in your body.

At the end of the proposal, the agreement was sealed with a drink of wine. Then the groom would say to the bride, "I am going to prepare a place for you," and he would leave.

When he finished the new addition to his father's house, the groom would return with all his groomsmen. They would come into the village blowing a horn. The brides in waiting would wonder, "Is it me? Is my groom coming for me?" The groom would take her back to the new home off his family's house and there they would celebrate the wedding for seven days.

Joe said *okay* as an act of faith. His faith came from a simple trust, a trust that even in a world he couldn't always say *yes* to, in times of challenge, pain, and struggle, times when he only had *okay*, Joe trusted that God was, is, and would be, *Semper Fi*, always faithful.

Where in your life have you only been saying, *no*? Where in your life has a *yes* been far removed and absent? Where in your life do you need the power of *okay* to set you free?

Name each place, offer it to God, and say, "So be it."

Chapter Five

*Well the South side of Chicago
Is the baddest part of town
And if you go down there
You better just beware
Of a man named Leroy Brown...
... bad, bad Leroy Brown*
Jim Croce

The Problem

There was a time in my life when life was simple, when my world was very clear, morality was never confusing, and a good day's work proved a good day's reward. As a child, *good* and *bad* were not mysterious because my mother and father were near and ever-ready, ever-present, ever-prepared to tell me what was *good* and what was *bad*.

Good things were: eating my vegetables, doing my homework, reading a book instead of watching television, saying, "Yes ma'am," "Yes sir," "Please," and "Thank you," bringing home E's on my report card (for Excellent, not the grade below D), making my bed and cleaning my room (or at least putting my dirty clothes away), taking my dishes to the sink and saying, "Thank you for dinner," (regardless of whether or not I was thankful). All these were good things.

Bad things were also very clear: yelling at my sister, talking back to my parents (saying "But...," "Why..," or "No..," instead of "Yes ma'am," or "Yes sir,") saying dirty words, saying, "Yuck," at dinner, hiding my brussel sprouts in my napkin, and the worst bad of all, according to my mother and sisters, was not lifting the lid, or if I did bother to lift the lid, not putting it back down when I was finished. (I didn't think it was my fault if none of the women in my house looked first before they went to the bathroom at night.)

As a child, *good* and *bad* were quite clear, and so were the results.

My parents taught me, "In life, do good things, and you'll be rewarded." For example, "Study hard, you'll get good grades. Practice hard, you'll win the game. And work hard and you'll get paid." My parents also told me, "Do bad things, you'll be punished, and what's more, you'll find only trouble, and life won't go well for you." For example, "Don't study, you'll flunk. Don't practice, you won't win the game. And don't work hard, and you'll be poor."

My parents not only taught me, they showed me. They rewarded me when I did well. They gave me praise, allowance, or privileges for jobs well done. They even judged me in a positive light. They told their friends, "He's such a good boy. He never causes any trouble."

They also punished me when I broke the rules. I was sent to my room. I got a spanking. (That was before anyone told parents that spanking was bad.) In our house, bad words were considered dirty, and mom's punishment was literally washing out our mouths with soap. You had to stick your tongue out and she rubbed soap over it. She did this for my own good, to teach me that bad words and bad actions lead to punishment. I was also judged in a negative light, "Why are you so bad?"

Mom and Dad had help from the church. At church, God was on the side of parents. I was taught that even if mom or dad can't see you, God can see you. I learned that Jesus watched me and didn't like it when I did bad. The second verse of *Jesus Loves Me* reminded me, "Jesus loves me when I'm bad, though it makes him very sad. Jesus loves me when I'm good, when I do the things I should." Though Jesus loves me when good or bad, according to the song, clearly bad made him sad. I was also told that, God, on the other hand, didn't get sad when we were bad, but instead God got mad. Promises of punishment, now or eternal, constantly loomed over me.

Though it may sound rough, actually it wasn't. It was in many ways wonderful, a simpler world of mom, dad, church, and apple pie, a world where what was good and what was bad was very clear, a world where consequences made sense, a world where you do good and you are rewarded, a world where you do bad and are punished, a world where God was on the side of parents and the police. A simpler time...

Then I grew up. The problem I uncovered was that the world described to me by my mom, dad, and the church wasn't always the world I experienced.

Once in a while during my teenage years, I saw bad choices result in bad consequences. A friend did drugs and was arrested. That made sense. But then there was a girl I was infatuated with who got cancer. She was, as far as all could tell, a good girl, but something bad happened. I asked, "Why her? What did she do?" No one could explain it to me.

In college, I volunteered at a local children's home. Many of the children had been physically and sexually abused. What did they do? They were, after all, only children.

Then I read the gospels as an adult. Though the church I grew up in had lucid definitions for *good* and *bad* people and behaviors, I saw a lack of clarity in Jesus.

Luke 15:*[1]Now all the tax collectors and sinners were coming near to listen to him. [2] And the Pharisees and the scribes were grumbling and saying, "This fellow welcomes sinners and eats with them."*

Labeling others, especially in terms of *good* and *bad,* was the pattern of the religious institutions and leaders of Jesus' day but not Jesus. Jesus refused and refuted labels of *good* or *bad* for others, and for himself.

Mark 10: [17] *...a man ran up and knelt before (Jesus), and asked him, "Good Teacher, what must I do to inherit eternal life?" [18] Jesus said to him, "Why do you call me good? No one is good but God alone.*

Jesus rejected the label of *good* for himself and said not to apply *good* to anyone but God. In this encounter, Jesus seems to doubt whether the man (and also us) would recognize *good* if we saw it.

As I read the gospels, Jesus didn't label people *good* or *bad.* The only label Jesus seems to have had for people is the label God had for him at his baptism, *beloved.*

Consider the difference between how Jesus treated Thomas in the following passage and how we've treated him ever since.

The Text

John 20: [19] When it was evening on that day, the first day of the week, and the doors of the house where the disciples had met were locked for fear of the Jews, Jesus came and stood among them and said, "Peace be with you." [20] After he said this, he showed them his hands and his side. Then the disciples rejoiced when they saw the Lord. [21] Jesus said to them again, "Peace be with you. As the Father has sent me, so I send you." [22] When he had said this, he breathed on them and said to them, "Receive the Holy Spirit. [23] If you forgive the sins of any, they are forgiven them; if you retain the sins of any, they are retained."

[24] But Thomas (who was called the Twin), one of the twelve, was not with them when Jesus came. [25] So the other disciples told him, "We have seen the Lord." But he said to them, "Unless I see the mark of the nails in his hands, and put my finger in the mark of the nails and my hand in his side, I will not believe."

[26] A week later his disciples were again in the house, and Thomas was with them. Although the doors were shut, Jesus came and stood among them and said, "Peace be with you." [27] Then he said to Thomas, "Put your finger here and see my hands. Reach out your hand and put it in my side. Do not doubt but believe." [28] Thomas answered him, "My Lord and my God!" [29] Jesus said to him, "Have you believed because you have seen me? Blessed are those who have not seen and yet have come to believe."

I feel sorry for Thomas. One bad day and two thousand years later, he's still paying for it. Thomas doubted (*bad*), and so Thomas was a *bad* person, a doubter. Thomas did *bad* and was *bad*. So, we tell our children, "Don't be like Thomas. Don't be a doubting Thomas." In our limited view, we condemn, label, and punish, and for many, like Thomas, our punishment shows no possibility of parole.

Yet, Jesus seems to have known something more. Jesus seems to have understood something different, something beyond *good* and *bad*, another view, another perspective which allowed him to give people like Thomas, people like us, grace, mercy, and hope. We need such a vision, such a word, a magic word...

Sometimes

The Text Revisited

Consider how the disciples, and we, might have treated Thomas if we had known the word *sometimes*...

John 20: [25...] *So the other disciples told him, "We have seen the Lord." But (Thomas) said to them, "Unless I see the mark of the nails in his hands, and put my finger in the mark of the nails and my hand in his side, I will not believe."*

They replied, "That's okay Thomas, *sometimes* bad is a pathway to good, sometimes doubt is the pathway to faith."

And ever since, parents and Sunday School teachers have taught children the story of Thomas saying, "Be like Thomas for his doubt was a pathway to faith."

Transformation

When I was growing up, as I said, *good* and *bad* were very clear. They were opposites. *Good* was the opposite of *bad*. *Bad* was the opposite of *good*. That's still often true. But *sometimes, bad* isn't the opposite of *good*. *Sometimes bad* is the pathway to *good*.

We've always labeled Thomas as *bad*, doubt as *bad*, doubt as the opposite of faith. Sometimes that is true... What Jesus understood about Thomas, about the disciples, and about us is that *sometimes bad* isn't the opposite of *good*, but the pathway to *good*.

In Thomas' case, doubt wasn't the opposite of faith, but the road to faith. Jesus helped him along the way. Jesus understood, *sometimes* doubt isn't the opposite of faith, *sometimes* doubt is the road to faith. I have many people in my congregation who have come through doubts to get to faith. I find that doubting is often quite helpful.

When I graduated from seminary, I was looking for a youth ministry position. While interviewing with a church in Atlanta, I was asked, "We have a youth in our church who is struggling with doubt. How do you feel about doubting?"

I replied, "I think doubting is wonderful. I don't think doubt is the opposite of faith. I think apathy is the opposite of faith. I find that doubt can be a great pathway to a mature faith."

Have you ever been in a job interview when, after the answer of a single question, you knew the interview was over? I have. Several times. That was one of them.

I stick by my answer. I think that *sometimes* doubt can be a pathway to faith.

I also find that *sometimes* shows up in the journeys of many people in our congregation.

Sometimes...
Sometimes doubt is the opposite of faith, but sometimes doubt can be a pathway to faith.

Sometimes weakness is the opposite of strength, but sometimes weakness can be the pathway to strength.

Sometimes addiction is the opposite of sobriety, but sometimes addiction can be the pathway to sobriety.

Sometimes infidelity is the opposite of fidelity, but sometimes infidelity can be a pathway to fidelity.

Sometimes failure is the opposite of success, but sometimes failure can be the pathway to success.

People are often paradoxical, like in this philosophical puzzle:

There once was a man who tried to fail and did. So, did he succeed or fail?

Obviously, there is no 'right' answer to this question for if he's trying to fail and succeeds then he didn't truly fail. In the same way, when trying to sort through a behavior and label it *good* or *bad*, the answer is impossible without knowing the outcome because *sometimes* bad is a pathway to good. And what is even more, for some of us, often the darker road is the only road. For some of us, *doubt is the only pathway to faith, weakness the only path to strength, addiction the only path to sobriety, infidelity the only path to fidelity, and failure the only path to success.*

For some of us, the dark path home is the only way we can find. For some of us, there is no other way. History agrees. Consider the following people, all people we would consider great, who in their own way understood that failure is not only a pathway to success, but many times the only pathway to success.

Abraham Lincoln had a stream of failures. He started a business in 1831 and failed. He ran for legislature in 1832 and lost. He started another business in 1836 and failed. He ran for elector in 1840 and lost. He ran for Congress in 1843 and 1848 and lost. He ran for the Senate in 1855 and lost. He then lost in a run for the Vice Presidency in 1856 and then again for the Senate in 1858. You wonder why the fellow got out of bed after all those losses. Yet, even after all that defeat, he succeeded in winning the presidency, emancipating slaves, and reuniting the nation symbolized today by our language. Before Lincoln we said, "The United States are..." but after Lincoln, we say, "The United States is...," one nation, singular. Regarding failure, Lincoln said, "My great concern is not whether you have failed, but whether you are content with your failure."

Thomas Edison's teachers said he was "too stupid to learn anything." He was fired from his first two jobs for being "non-productive." As an inventor, Edison made 1,000 unsuccessful attempts at inventing the light bulb. When a reporter asked, "How did it feel to fail 1,000 times?" Edison refused to hear of it. He didn't consider those attempts as failure at all. Edison replied, "I didn't fail 1,000 times. The light bulb was an invention with 1,000 steps." Concerning his other inventions and their steps, "I have not failed. I've just found 10,000 ways that won't work."

Henry Ford failed and went broke five times before he succeeded. Regarding failure Ford said, "Failure is simply the opportunity to begin again, this time more intelligently."

Walt Disney was fired by a newspaper editor because "he lacked imagination and had no good ideas." He went bankrupt several times before he built Disneyland. In fact, the proposed park was rejected by the city of Anaheim on the grounds that it would only attract riffraff. "You may not realize it when it happens," Disney said later, "but a kick in the teeth may be the best thing in the world for you."

Winston Churchill failed sixth grade. He was subsequently defeated in every election for public office until he became Prime Minister at the age of 62. Regarding failure, he said, "Never give in, never give in, never, never, never, never - in nothing, great or small, large or petty - never give in except to convictions of honor and good sense. Never, never, never, never give up."

Albert Einstein did not speak until he was four years old and did not read until he was seven. His parents thought he was "sub-normal," and one of his teachers described him as "mentally slow, unsociable, and adrift forever in foolish dreams." He was expelled from school and was refused admittance to the Zurich Polytechnic School. He did eventually learn to speak and read. Even to do a little math. Regarding failure, Einstein said, "It's not that I am so smart, it's just that I stay with problems longer."

Carlton Fisk, former catcher who played for both the Boston Red Sox and Chicago White Sox summed up the attitude of all the leaders and visionaries I just mentioned, "It's not what you achieve. It's what you overcome. That's what defines you career." And your life.

Sometimes failure is the opposite of success, but for all these people mentioned above, people who changed the world, for them failure was simply part of their journey toward success. So it was with Thomas, doubt was the necessary pathway he needed to faith.

When Thomas touched Jesus and believed... Jesus responded, "Have you believed because you have seen me? Blessed are those who have not seen and yet have come to believe." Jesus seems to be speaking to more than Thomas, to others in the future, to us, who would one day read, "Blessed are you when you have not seen yet believed." This is a blessing for all of us on our different paths because Jesus understood *sometimes.* Jesus' vision was important two thousand years ago and is important today, for Thomas and those of us like him who need the darker path toward home.

My hope is that the church will pick up Jesus' blessing and offer it with the same compassion.

Blessed are you when you don't have to go through doubt to faith, but if you do, then welcome home. *Sometimes* that's what it takes to get here...

Blessed are you when you don't have to go through skepticism in order to have some sense of certainty in your life, but if you do, then welcome home. *Sometimes* that's what it takes to get here...

Blessed are you when you don't have to go through depression in order to have peace in your life, but if you do, then welcome home. *Sometimes* that's what it takes to get here...

Blessed are you when you don't have to go through infidelity to find fidelity, but if you do, then welcome home. *Sometimes* that's what it takes to get here...

Blessed are you when you don't have to go through gluttony to have contentment, but if you do, then welcome home. *Sometimes* that's what it takes to get here...

Blessed are you when you don't have to go through alcoholism or drug addition to find sobriety in your life, but if you do, then welcome home. *Sometimes* that's what it takes to get here...

Sometimes, we all need blessings, we all need the grace to find our way.

How do you need the grace of *sometimes?*

Is there someone you've been treating as a Doubting Thomas who needs grace from you today? Why not give it?

Conclusion

Do you believe in magic?
The Lovin' Spoonful

Three umpires were asked, "How do you call balls and strikes?"
The first said, "I call them as I see them."
The second said, "I call them as they are."
But the third said, "They are as I call them."

In your life, you are the third umpire. Your life is as you call it.

If you say, "More!" then you'll constantly be on the search for the next thing, chasing a hunger which grows the more it feeds, providing a continuous, relentless, eternal dissatisfaction. And if you say, "If only...," or look for something else constantly, then your life is already lessened, and you'll continue to be disgruntled, wanting the world to change for your pleasure or comfort.

However, if you claim your power, owning the reality that your life is as you call it, if you say definitively, "*Enough*," then contentment and joy are not far away. If you can add to *enough* and say, "Ahhh...," then you will enjoy each moment for what it is, not looking to the next, but living the present as a gift, a wonderful, delightful, magical gift.

If you label life, experiences, and people as only *good* or *bad*, then you will find life one frustration after another and be only disappointed in yourself, in others, and in God.

However, if you can see potential in yourself and others knowing that *sometimes* doubt can be a pathway to faith, *sometimes* weakness can be the pathway to strength, *sometimes* addiction can be the pathway to sobriety, *sometimes* infidelity can be a pathway to fidelity, and *sometimes* failure can be the pathway to success, then your life will always be open to new possibilities, and you will look at yourself and others with hope.

If you can refrain from saying, "No!" to the painful parts of your life, but instead face your potentially overwhelming challenges, finding strength from deep inside your soul, and muster an accepting, *"Okay,"* then your life will be open to the miraculous joys and new life God can bring from even the worst injustice, tragedy, and loss.

If you can take a step further, letting go of *good* and *bad,* trusting that only God knows what is ultimately *good* and *bad* in the world and in your life, and open yourself to each moment as something that *may be* one of the best things that has happened to you and for you, through you and for others, then you will expect any moment to be potentially life giving, and even death itself will be seen with hopeful expectation.

And finally, if you can claim all these words: *enough, ahhh, okay, maybe,* and *sometimes,* then you will find that you and your experience of the world will be transformed.

You are the third umpire. The world is waiting for you to speak, to call it, to see it as you say.

So, wait no more. Move forward in your life. Wave your hand at the doors in front of you and say, *"Open sesame."*

Made in the USA
Charleston, SC
09 December 2011